Treasure Walks
Connections, Observations and Reflections

Treasure Walks
Connections, Observations and Reflections

Prasanta Behera

BLACK EAGLE BOOKS
2020

BLACK EAGLE BOOKS

USA address:
7464 Wisdom Lane
Dublin, OH 43016

India address:
E/312, Trident Galaxy, Kalinga Nagar,
Bhubaneswar-751003, Odisha, India

E-mail: info@blackeaglebooks.org
Website: www.blackeaglebooks.org

First International Edition Published by
BLACK EAGLE BOOKS, 2020

Treasure Walks
by **Prasanta Behera**

Edited By: **Charlie Moynahan**

Original Copyright © **Suparna Behera**

All proceeds from Treasure Walk will be go to Black Eagle Books - A nonprofit endeavor to propagate Indian literature globally.

All rights reserved. No part of this publication may be reproduced, stored in a retrieval system, or transmitted, in any form or by any means, electronic, mechanical, photocopying, recording or otherwise without the prior permission of the publisher.

Cover image by: Prasanta Behera
Back cover image by: Ishani Behera

Cover & Interior Design: Ezy's Publication

ISBN- 978-1-64560-081-7 (Paperback)
Library of Congress Control Number: 2020940112

Printed in United States of America

To my wife, Suparna (Tikli)

for the treasure walk
around the sacred fire
on a cold december night
to start the new journey
and continuing it...

Contents

Introduction	9
Chapter 1: Treasure Walks	
Treasure Walks	15
Textured Wind	17
Stone in Sand	19
Park Bench	20
Walking on the same street	21
End of the Trail	22
Unforgotten	23
Stranger in homeland	24
Silent Notes	25
Chapter 2: Memories	
Pineapple	29
Band-Aid	30
Sweet sixteen	31
Becoming "21"	32
Gramophone	34
Lunch Bag	36
Lost Poet	38
One Minute	40
Unspoken words	41
Wall of Love	42
Sound of Father	43
Inheritance	44
Fish Curry	46
Selfless Act	47
Power of Silence	48
My Father	50
Phone Call	52
Memory & Experience	54
Patterns	55
Midnight Poetry	57
Third eye	59
Best Gift	61

Chapter 3: Observations

Graduate	65
Community	66
Thoughts on Covid-19	67
Airport	69
Clue	70
Same Date	71
Summer Afternoon	72
Wave	73
Destination	74
Returned	75
Anger	76
Birthday	77
Death in Bed	78
Mind	79
Thoughts	80
Buddha	81

Chapter 4: Thoughts

Collection of one-minute thoughts	85

Chapter 5: Reflections

Sunrise at Mt. Umunhum	119
Mt Whitney	120
Mount Kilimanjaro	121
Persimmon Tree	122
Water Connection	123
Window	125
Beyond the end point	126
Traditions	127
Celebrations: Circle of Life (Nuakhai)	129
Poetry & Wine	131
River banks	132
Line in the sand	134
Strange Number	135
Life	136
Basket of Prayers	137
God of Experience	138
Dilemma	139
Engraved Thoughts	141
Audience of One	142
Poetic winter	143
Atheist	144
A Letter to Myself	146

Introduction

We walk.
We walk alone.
We walk with friends.
We walk with strangers.
We walk with family members.
We will walk till the end.
We walk.

Some of those walks remain in the heart and remind us of memories of connections, it allows us to carry our journey from today to tomorrow. I have captured some of them as "Treasure Walks".

The book is divided into three themes: The first two chapters are reflections of connections. Connections to people; connections which are important in life but we take it for granted often. In the last book ("Mystery of Leaves") and here, I continue to stitch those connections with poems. This is my humble attempt.

Observations, unnoticed before but now more conscious like water droplets in a fountain to watching a boy in the airport, I have captured some of those in Chapter 3. In Chapter 4, I started with the idea of observing deeply on a specific frame. Those initial thoughts from the observations became my "on-minute" thought series. The first minute says it all - whether you are watching a modern painting or meeting someone, with eyes open or closed.

Chapter 5 is reflections of oneself as I continue this journey. I have shared mine not to influence but make you feel like the breeze you hear sitting in the middle of a bamboo garden. Find your tune; find your voice.

Some of the concepts like mountains, deserts, waves, red & yellow leaves ... are repeated in many poems. In one sense it shows my limitations but in another sense these are elements which connect and strengthen my connections. I cannot avoid it; all my poems are built on those key elemental thoughts - rooted deeply in my heart.

My hope is that when you read the poems, you feel, reflect and connect with yourself.

- Prasanta

Afternoon twilight
scattered yellow and red leaves
treasure walk in silence
path unknown.

Fall 2018

Treasure Walks

Treasure Walks

Like songs you like to hear again and again
like places you like to visit again and again
walks, that happened, you like to do it again
walks, enveloped with memories and emotions
treasure walks, they are
sprinkled along in the past
buried deep inside my heart.

[Walking in the field]
If there is a walk where you feel like a king
if there is a walk where you feel safe
for a young boy, it was always in my village
navigating the rice fields with a cane
humming a tune, touching rice grains
stopping once in a while to gaze the view
green rice fields between two mountains.
We cross many fields, all shapes, and sizes
square, rectangles bounded by ridges
when I could not cross a big stream,
grandfather, you carried me with your might
I cannot forget those walks; the shadow still lasts.

[a walk as an adult]
We walked in spurts over the years
your long shadows dwarfed mine growing up
we talked and did not at the same time
years passed by like a windowless frame
one day, we walked together sharing the loss
the big shadow of yesteryear melted down with few tears
we hugged, walked again slowly, down the memory lane
father, finally we walked together as friends.

[a walk around fire]
We walked around a fire on a cold December night
strangers became partners for life overnight
I have been walking with you since that day
have not forgotten my promise till today
walked in beaches and many desert parks
it doesn't matter where we walk
I will keep walking with you till last breath.

[a walk in the park]
Afternoon twilight
scattered yellow and red leaves
I listened to your words one by one
walking in the park and sidewalks.
Layered emotions between laughters
I struggled with the chained moments
connected thoughts from past to present
I am glad that we walked again.

[a walk alone]
Alone I must walk
to listen to the mountain's silence
to see the moon's reflection in one's darkness
to listen to the thoughts crossing my mind
to let the winds tell stories
walk I must with my shadow till the end.

December 2018

Textured Wind

[morning]
Wind blowing silently from the east
swirling, twisting around the bamboo trees
silence interspersed with fluttering leaves
bamboo clusters dancing with the wind
an orchestra for this stranger to feel
textured wind from the bamboo trees.

[afternoon]
A boat silently glides in the lake
slicing the water, splashing waves
submerged dead tree stumps standing
scattered along, remnants of past,
cormorants on top, watching across
guardians of the lake for generations
wind blows, waves criss-cross each other
few drops nourish the soul of this traveler
textured wind from the water;
let it continue a few minutes longer.

[evening]
Rain dances with the wind
sputtering along the roads, uneven
water droplets streaks in car window
forming patterns; flattens and coagulates
watching the forms, a traveler I am
patterns of life framed and unframed
texture wind in the windowpane.

[reflection]

Textured wind in bamboo trees
textured wind in splashing waves
textured wind in water droplets
hidden beauty in patterns and melodies
life is like the wind
textured by people we meet
textured by people we love.

January 2019
A day in Kerala, India while vacationing.

Stone in Sand

Pick up the stone as you walk in the sand
pick up as you try to reach the end
the stones are from the days of yore
it may be of dinosaurs or life long before
each tells a story of journeys taken
some smooth and some shaken.
I cannot tell you which one to choose
hundreds lie along the path of view
some hidden and some calling for you
Feel the wave in your feet
feel the warmth of the sunset
let your shadow grow longer
as you walk on your path a bit longer
wondering why the stones matter.

I gave you two stones long before
when we walked together on the beach
you did not know the journey it had taken
you were too young to think for a second,
you threw one into the ocean
gave me the other to do the same
I told you it will come back when you grow up
all the love contained from yesteryears
I am not walking with you this time
but do pick up a stone from the sand
feel it; let it go back to the ocean again
to come back again with memories.
The stone you gave me long before
reminds me of the path we have taken
I have left it on your desk now
For you to throw back into the ocean.

October   2018

Park Bench

Redwood, Rhus Ridge, Los Trancos,
Edgewood, Russian Ridge, Sanborn
pearls along the Bay Area ridge trail
parks, we have walked for hours
afternoon sunlight playing hide and seek.
Did you notice the stones along the trail
the colors of flowers scattered along the trail
the tall grass dancing with the winds
giant redwood trees rising to the sky
the birds singing on treetops
squirrels coming in and out of shades,
a lonely bench on the viewpoint
where friends become strangers
strangers become friends
shared thoughts linger in the veil
I am the observer and the observed
walking in the park trails ...oblivious.

July 2019

Walking on the same street

I walked alone on the same street yesterday
which we used to walk every Tuesday,
crossing the busy street until the roads meet
afternoon sun shining bright.
I walked alone between the shades
with fall leaves sprinkled along the way.

Rows of houses with gardens in-front
beautiful flowers welcomed all
But I seem to be lost
unfazed by the glorious flowers
as there was no one to share.
I walked alone on the same street
which we used to do every week.

What we talked on those walks
I do not remember a tidbit of that
Maybe it was the long silences
broken by a few sentences
or the sudden stop to smell the flowers.
All that I remember is that
the flowers spoke
the fall leaves crinkled
when we walked on the same street
on Tuesday of each week.

October 2017

End of the Trail

Hundreds of trails I have hiked
many have befriended and speak
birds roaming in skies, silent with watchful eyes
squirrels laying the open nuts along the sides.
Each trail is unique, named and unnamed
TonyLook, Limekiln, Priest rock, Black Mountain
veins of the mountain; awaiting in silence.
Most of the time, it is a hike from start to finish
walking along, enjoying the view with pain and a smile.
Sometimes when a fork comes in the path of journey
unknown, unframed signpost, a decision lingers in mind.
Is it the craziness in me or the poetry of Frost?
I like to venture in the unmarked trail a bit more
go to some distance and see what lies ahead
there must be something good, a hiker's joy!

Strolling in a park with friends in spring
a small lake and few trails leading to hills
saw a trail signpost labeled "Trail ends in Bench"
For some, it was clearly a trail of a perfect match
a small walk, a bench at the end to rest and enjoy.
Yet, I pondered what makes this trail unique
a narrow path leading up to a small hill;
a single wooden bench under the cypress tree
to sit and watch the blue sky or stars at night.
An emblem glued in the middle of the bench
few words of loving memory left behind by a friend.
I wonder if we all need a bench at the end of the day
to quieten the thoughts, view the sky, smell the flowers
reminiscence the love sprinkled along life's trail
in the end, only an emblem will remain
for the next hiker to enjoy the moment!

May 2019

Unforgotten

Cold winter morning
fog of darkness layered
dancing moon whispering
uneven roads, bumbling ride
time seems slow and fast - juxtaposed
anxious moments, constrained thoughts
tired body, smile in the heart
the sudden touch, the lean in
the warm breath, the sensation
never felt before, a new beginning.

A moment
still etched in memory
still etched in the heart.
it is not forgotten
it is there, it will be there
in the labyrinth of thoughts.

July 2017

Stranger in homeland

Where are the dusts that covered the path
the broken pots sprinkled like a painter's art
the morning smoke from the thatched huts
the jingle bell of cows and goats
the children who played with balls of straw
the old faces who sat under the tree
smoking pipe, telling stories of old and wise.

All those memories of the past, I see no more
strolling across the narrow path from days of yore.
The roads are cleaner, no small stream to cross over
the jingles are gone, the children stay home alone
The roots of the banyan tree hang low
old faces have become ghosts
no more stories to be told.

An air of strangeness breaths inside
no one seems to notice of my stride;
unlike days of before, my presence is no uproar,
the faces are hidden, piercing eyes gleam unbidden.
How can I convince this is my stead
the dust of old still bled
I am no stranger of this realm
I also danced here in the summer rain.

I have become a stranger.
I have become a stranger
of my own land
to myself again!

April 2018

Silent Notes

A boat silently glides in water
you try to touch the ripples.
Bamboo trees swing with the wind
you close your eyes to breathe in.
Desert flowers stretch between hills
you carefully walk in the midst
bending often, framing pictures.
Thousands of birds in the wildlife refuge
you count how many you can name.

I see you taking notes silently
clicking your phone with one finger;
few pauses and glances in between.
You look around with a faint smile
few more clicks and a sigh of relief.
I ask you to share what you wrote
you simile, "random stuff", you say.
I am left anxious to know
the captured thoughts of the day.

Unknown words locked in sprinkled thoughts
few slip by when we converse between silences
and some I can sense, between smiles and fulfilled eyes.
I have threaded a few of those moments in my poems
I hope you can discover them.

Cormorants sitting on top of dead tree stumps
watchful eyes as we glide across the river
I love to observe you in those silent moments.

May 2019

Memories

Pineapple

Sitting alone in the kitchen island
you feel like a king unclaimed;
a crown on top and flat bottom to rock
your presence is felt often
to all who pass by your land.
The thorns and scales in your body
arranged like a beautiful melody;
like pinching rains of summer
I feel when I touch your armor.

When I see you standing alone in the island
it reminds me a voice I have not forgotten
she loves your sweetness like no other
and I learned to love your thorns like feather
I laugh at my struggle with each cut
I am getting better, believe it or not.
O! Sweet king of unclaimed land!
let me hear that voice again.

August 2018

Band-Aid

Lately, I notice, I keep cutting myself
while slicing a cucumber or carving a pineapple
or when opening a can or fixing broken equipment.
My wife tells me every time to be careful
but four out of ten, I end up in the same fate;
most of the time I do not tell anyone
but when I get caught, I get reminded again
"You are worse than your children."
"Nothing to worry about, it happens", I say
show the cut finger properly wrapped
a paper napkin, all that is needed.

I was cutting a pineapple last December
slicing the skin like a master woodcutter
got distracted and a finger got cut
before I could hide it, I got caught
my daughter said, "Dad, I can't believe you did it again,"
she rushed to get a band-aid and medicine
I told her not to tell her mom
or else no pineapple for three months.
Last month she moved to her own apartment
empty nesters life begins again
what will I do now if I get a cut again
putting the band-aid will never be same
I promise to be careful going forward
when you visit next time, pineapple slices
will be waiting in circles and squares.

January 2019

Sweet sixteen

When I saw a dimple in your babycheek
I knew your smile is to keep
Your hair was so curly
combing, not to be taken lightly
looked golden, in the afternoon sun
walking, stopping in Malibu beach often
filling the yellow bucket with shells
sands all over your hand and smiling face
trails of the small footprint left behind
memories remain, intact with time.

The little girl grew up fast
kisses became hugs
sweet voices became sweeter
trinket became sound of a dancer
words become wiser
the young girl became a big sister
still, sweetness remained.
I wait for you every summer
To tell you the scary funny stories
hear your laugh with all its glories
I read your essays on trips taken
sometimes I cannot understand
words are smaller than an ant.

Now you are sweet sixteen
blossoming from a teen,
go out to the world and make a change
remember what your grandparents say
"We grow stronger when we water our roots."
I look forward to a hug every time we meet
my blessings will always be with you
today is your day, enjoy it in every way!

December 2018

Becoming "21"

Now that you are Twenty-one
you can drink wine like anyone
but that is not why we celebrate "21"
It is a point where roads ahead are empty
It is a point where all possibilities exist
It is a point where vastness becomes reality
It is a point where love comes softly
It is a point where dreams become a force
It is a point where life becomes a racecourse
It is a point where memories of past fly like a bird
It is a point where we cling dearly to the feathers of the past
It is a point where we stand facing each other
Yes, son, you have reached that point at last.
The roads not taken are to be taken
The dust of old shoes is to be shaken
The broken paths to be mended
The silent voices need to be awakened.

The inner voice of "21" will say
Take me to a journey
    where dreamers meet
    where ideals are unchained
    where courage becomes love
    where love finds love
    where pursuit is a joy
    where paths unfold like a morning flower
    where memories of the past are still safe
    where the strings of love are still unbroken.
Take me there; a journey we will share.

The root is where strength comes
Mother is where all love emanates from
call her often to make the bond unshaken
that is the journey we all have taken.
Now, as for me, your father
we are friends and partners
a glass of wine and a hug is all I wish for.

December 2017

Gramophone

A strange box sat outside the front door
I scratched my head, what I ordered before
looking closer, it was not for me but for my son
I wondered what he has ordered in this big carton;
my inquisition came to surprise when he told in a cool voice
"a record player for me mistakenly sent to you, Dad"
"A record player? Do GenZ people use that?" I asked.
when everything is available for streaming
He said, "record players are back, you should try it"
I scratched my head and start thinking
It is weird, how things come back given some time,
nostalgic moments get revived.

Reminiscent thoughts of long before
raced in my mind as it happened just now.
It was a summer visit to my grandfather
when I was just a teenager,
during my summer trip.
He showed me his prized possession
a gramophone with a bighorn;
he showed me how it works,
with a smile, "It is yours", he said.
Handed me five old song records,
to play in the meantime.
They all sounded funny for a young boy
playing with it and listening was still a joy.

It was my toy possession for a year
cranking the handle and listening to old records
until my curious brother decides to take it apart
see how it works, unknowing how to put it back.

We tried to put it back many times in desperation
finally, hid the whole thing from mom,
it was from her father, we did not want to tell her,
I am sure she knew it, ignored it with a kinder heart.
The gramophone was gone, the records gathered dust
but the memory and love never got lost
I wish I could find the old vinyl records back again
pass it to my son, in case he wants to listen
I would like to listen to it too, dreaming in the old
memory lane.

December 2018

Lunch Bag

X-men, Superman, Avengers
Barbie, Wonder-Women, Ironman
Capt. America, Lilo, and Elastigirl.
Rows and rows of kids with lunch bags
walking, giggling and laughing
some in excitement with new friends
some not sure why summer came to an end.
I watched from my car at the stop
kids are walking one by one non-stop
some students are carrying the lunch bag
for some, the grandparents are holding
like a mighty weapon along with the backpack
for some parents, a tussle brewing
to hand that lunch bag to the kid is hesitating
the face of the kid tells the story
an ugly lunch bag, even I would not like to carry.
It was not long ago, I was packing lunch
Bagel bites, PBJ, apple, Go-Gurt and imaginations
First few years, the lunch bag had characters
after that, they said, "Dad, I have grown up.
I am not a kid anymore."
You need to up your creative game some more."
So, I packed lunch in a brown paper bag
so that they can keep inside their backpack.
Every day, I made some scribblings
smiley faces, squiggly faces and a quote in between.
Sometimes they asked me what the quote means
and sometimes they laugh at me.
I wished I had an iPhone at that time
it would have been easy to capture the lines

laugh now what crazy things I wrote at that time.
A flashing light and a mild horn,
wake up - all the kids have crossed the stop
I need to move forward, my imagination is shaken
but I have a smile in thoughts unspoken.

October 2018

Lost Poet

A bottle of wine and a card lay on the table
"Lost Poet", a red blend, perfect gift on this Father's day.
As I looked closely, the back label of the bottle says
"Wine is Poetry - write Yours".
So, I thought let me try a few lines as I sip and enjoy
best way to acknowledge.

[poem for the back]

Lost Poet
Standing in the desert between mirages
waiting for the night sky for the stars to tell,
I am the lone camel rider, blanched by twilight
will I be lost in the moonless night?

Looking to the waves gliding in the ocean
fragmented patterns, rising and collapsing
a glass bottle floats in the ocean
struggling to reach its destination
a small message engraved in the bottle
"What is lost, can be found."
I am also lost in the wave to be found.

A story-less traveler I was, traversing the realm
until I found few words from own's darkness
Many times I struggled and then I found you
thoughts from the deep, like stars of the night
showing the path in the moonless night
few thoughts got scribbled in poems.
You and I are the "Lost Poets", a journey taken
interspersed with silence between moments

[end of poem]

Next year's Father's Day gift may be different
what can be more interesting than a "Lost Poet" bottle
I hope it is not a waffle.

June 2019

One Minute

Every weekday when I go to the gym,
I stand on the same spot looking east
to watch spectacles of the sky unruffled
the blanched sunrise, the shredded clouds
the fluttering birds in the distance
a palm tree standing in silence.
A picture I take to capture the moment
everyday is different, each carries a frame
the view may not be glorious all the time
but I must look when I go every time
in the darkness of winter, in the sputtering rain
in the early light of summer,
in the fall with scattered leaves without complaint.

I do not pray to the sun God like my forebears of history
so, why I spend that minute beyond nature's beauty
I stand and let the thoughts float
to those whom I have promised before
I close my eyes and thank them all
some chant and some meditate,
I spent a few seconds, that's all.
When I look back at the pictures I have taken
each one reminds me of a path unbroken
we have evolved together, day after day
blended thoughts captured in frames.

December 2018

Unspoken words

Waiting for the right time
to say the words
for a new beginning
for a new life
to change the world
but foolish we all are
to wait for the right moment
when the moment is now
when words are in the heart
when life is in-front.

October 2016

Wall of Love

A small wall divided the two houses;
we were like monkeys,
instead of coming from the front,
we jumped over it when called;
it was a small wall after all.
Layers of bricks did not make it small,
it was your love;
we did not see any difference
between the houses growing up.

When I was sick or had an accident
you visited often.
When I hear your deep voice from upstairs
anticipation of questions was a nerve-racking affair;
"Be careful next time", you used to say
handing me a few books to read in bed.
A sigh of relief crossed my mind
when you touched my forehead to comfort me.
I knew there is much love behind that
I was glad about your visits each time.

We drifted apart across continents
our meetings have become intermittent;
the young boy became an adult and a father
yet I never felt a dip in that love from afar.
When I see you in rare events
the time in between shrinks in those moments
we start from where we left off, spoken or unspoken.
feels like coming home after a long time.
Words which seemed stuck while growing up
now comes freely without any hesitation;
there is no wall to jump, no anxiety of questions
we have marked our trails on our own terms.

March 2020

Sound of Father

Sitting alone in the backyard
on this dry summer afternoon,
I close my eyes to hear the sounds;
sounds of nature, sounds from nature,
sounds that remind of someone dear.

I can hear the sounds in my ear and imagination
sounds of the water drop from the fountain
sounds of crackling noise when walking on dried fall leaves
sounds of winds swirling around trees
sounds of thunder and rain on a summer afternoon
sounds of hummingbirds sucking nectar in garden
sounds of words spoken and unspoken
sounds of silence between breaths
sounds of silence between glances
sounds from faces, visible and faded;
what is the sound that reminds of my father,
I start to ruminate on this Father's Day.

I close my eyes and searched again
vibrations not measured in instruments.
I start to tap the chair handle and hum intermittently
suddenly, it reminded of my father and his father instantly,
tapping the chair, waiting anxiously for me to come home
that is the sound which connected all three generations
that is the sound when I make reminds of them;
now I do the same, carrying the sound ingrained.
I hope my son will discover it someday
like I have discovered it of my father today.

Father's Day, 2019

Inheritance

Like winds before rain, your presence felt
when you visited in rare events;
Looking up in awe, I wondered
if I could make the journey like yours;
crossing the oceans, to forge a new path
on my own.

I stumbled, struggled, wandered
navigating the new paths in-front
yet, your faith in me was never lost;
the spectator of yesteryears
stitched in your story over the years.
Three decades passed since the journey
sprinkled dust has covered the paths uncanny
time spent, roads traveled, stories shared,
life is richer from the love inherited.

I inherited the style of writing letter "E & F";
the distinct "E" and mirror image "F"
not sure if you have noticed yet.
I inherited a love of classical music
listening during our long rides from the back seat.
Now when I do the same in my long drives,
my kids switch to iPhones, I enjoy what I inherited.
I inherited the quest to know the scriptures
the path of knowledge with an open mind,
I have not struggled in my quest since then,
I am working on it, one word at a time.
I inherited the love of nature, since our first trip
hiking to the Vernal falls of Yosemite,

the traveler in me never got lost,
the inheritance opened my eyes over the years.
Of all the things I observed over the years
your definition of family and love to all
are a true reflection of yours,
It can not be inherited like others
yet over the years being near, influenced
I have inherited a few drops of that love.

I have inherited from you more than a son,
the burden is now on me to reflect on
pass the inheritance to the next generation
I keep none; experience all.

October 2019

Fish Curry

Every Wednesday, I wait for the text on WhatsApp
to come over for dinner, and I mostly do.
Between sips of red wine, we chat for hours
You do not sit, always in the kitchen on act.
Fresh vegetables from your garden sautéed
Grilled fish and salad, what else one can ask.

I enjoy your grilled salmon and Tilapia
But it is the mustard fish curry
that you make once in a while, I love the most;
reminds me of my mother when I taste it
It always came with love, imprinted in heart
I savor it slowly; no need to hurry.

The emptiness left behind few years ago
You have filled some of it with your love
I look forward to your text with eager
I will come for sure, fish or no fish.

October 2019

Selfless Act

We were both strangers across oceans
no relation, no connection, unknown to each other
yet a simple selfless act long ago
connected us, blending our lives forever;
an act which could have been forgotten
a connection created and lost
a kindness magnanimously ignored
but you did not let it happen;
not because of the signature on the paper
but for your love beyond oneself;
it has carried us together over the years
slowly entangling our memories
like the vines in your garden;
In every step of life, I have found both of you
in need and in celebrations
in the hospital to welcome the newborn
in the family get together connecting generations
in support of adventures of self discovery
in your garden, allowing to pick Persimmons,
You proudly say I am your son
never have I felt different from day one;
the paper which brought me here is lost now
not your love - not our connection
life has been richer from this nurtured existence;
no words can describe this beautiful experience
your selfless act has carried us to the distance.

April 2020

Power of Silence

Every Saturday, I waited for the phone to ring
few minutes of the call from afar is all in need
hope got renewed, links got stronger, voices got engraved
remained in the heart since then; fragmented yet unshaken
fight despair thoughts, when they come again.

The Mexican vase splintered in the darkness of oneself
I kept silent, truth untold, emptiness lingered in the veil,
you did not say anything knowing full well
now I understand the love in that silence.

I could not understand the power of your love
I could feel it, yet I did not embrace it well
Your love was pure; I myself was unsure, searching within
yet we marched on stitching one thread at a time.
There is a magic in your hug, the longer it is,
the better it gets
feel the power of your calmness, every-time I embrace;
hope renewed, life recharged, unknown becomes apparent
serenity enters like morning fog, soothing the voices within.

Days and years have passed since the phone calls
the connection has become stronger, voice ingrained
uncertainty of fog withered; the fabric of love strengthened
the boat of life pushed forward by your hug and love.
When the boat rocked again a few years ago
you held it steady, filling the void slowly
every step of the way, I felt the power
love and silence carried all of us forward.

Someone touches your feet, someone bows
I want a big long hug and a kiss on the forehead
to feel the power between the silent breaths
to feel the same calmness as the Mother's lap.
Now when you call, no need to announce
your voice is imprinted, I can imagine out
It has taken longer for me to understand,
we have crossed many mountains.
I am here, will be there whenever needed
your power of silence has taught me,
Mother's love in a new way.

November 2019

My Father

The best picture I remember of you
it was off when you were twenty-six
black and white, lanky self with a smile
a cigarette between the fingers
"Laugh - That's life", you wrote on the white border
you have not stopped sharing your laughter
even when times were harder.

Your shadow was too big to measure growing up
your anger was one to be reckoned with
yet your love was transparent like sunlight
comforting, even in tumultuous times.
Sitting between you and mom every Sunday
morning tea was a ritual where we connected
the anticipation of a chemistry question lurked always;
Imprinted memories remain.
Now when I ask such a question to my son, get a reply,
"Dad, you are asking too many questions."

You traveled distances to make ends meet
never said no to any family members in need
yet you (and Mom) were happy with limited resources
even-though struggling often to meet month's end;
I never felt insecure at any moment.
You welcomed home anyone remotely connected
love of homeland, love for family was more than self
something I realize the value, in this individualistic age.

You returned to your homeland after retirement
stirred the thinking, connected old and the new generation
no medal hangs; yet everyone knows a true son of the land.
For me, you the same father who carried me to the hospital
after each scooter accident or cut from jumping wire
you are the same father; did not give up when I stumbled
faith in me kept me going, we marched each step together.
I may not have achieved much - but it does not matter
the journey of life has taught me a lot more.

"Chemistry - that's life", you used to say
yet, I did not follow your path, crossed oceans
for the journey of my own making with your blessings
unfathomable distance divided us for years
letters, calls and occasional visits connected us,
yet the power of love never subsides us.
Now your grandson is dusting your path
we have come full circle, at last.

The long shadow of past years have melted away
the distance between father and son washed away
we walked together often navigating past and present
hearing your stories, observing your spiritual strength
"Laugh - that's life", you have truly embodied well
Father - we have walked together with stories to tell.

December 2019

Phone Call

The first time I called the phone rang,
before we could speak, connection ended;
a costly affair to make calls across oceans.
it was long before mobile and the internet.

The second time I called, your hostel warden said
you were not there, gone to college;
we were strangers on two continents.

The third time I called, perseverance paid off,
looking at the walls, between the holes and squiggly lines
few words started flowing interspersed with long silences.

The fourth time I called, you laughed, faintly
I must have said something crazy
that is what you say, I don't remember.

The fifth time I called, we talked about plans
we were still strangers, waiting to be partners;
distance seems a bit shorter, still unsure of each other.

Few more calls followed; laughter got a bit bolder
an air of comfort seeped in, like easterly winds
we were still strangers in-waiting, a journey in-making.

A vow in-front of fire in a cold December night
featherlight emotions floating with sunrise
carving slowly the unknown each moment
a clear path in front; an anxious heart gladden.

Thirty years have passed since the first call
a journey taken, promises kept and few broken
now, we are not strangers, yet I am still discovering
In the rare phone calls, I receive between meetings,
once in awhile I make you laugh, you say,
"You are still crazy as the day we met"
I am okay with it; we are here together and that's all it matters.

August 2019

Memory & Experience

"You do not remember anything",
my wife reminds me quite often,
when I miss identifying gifts I have given or gotten.
I say I must be getting old, memory is failing
a quick answer to bypass the investigative questioning.
Even if I had the memory power of my younger days
I hope I do not remember any gifts I have given
nor should you ask me that question, I rarely keep track of them.
When I was young, I could recite long poems
to impress the teacher, friends and my parents.
now I question, what is a memory after all?
bytes of information stored in my brain if I can recall.
I do not remember lines of poems beyond a few fragments
I do not I remember stats of many past events
nor can I recite long verses from scriptures
fragmented memories - why do I need them?

I do not remember the color of your gift
nor do I remember what it may have been
but I do remember the shared thoughts
the moments, experiences - blurred yet visible
like a boat navigating foggy waters
like an unmarked page of a book
like a floating leaf falling from a tree
like the evening sunrise from the Pacific
like the dew on a flower, trickling down to the inner self
they are there all the time,
surfacing once in a while, when the moment is right.
Yet, it may happen they will remain there until the end
few of them, I have converted to poems
that is my return gift from the shared experience

May 2019

Patterns

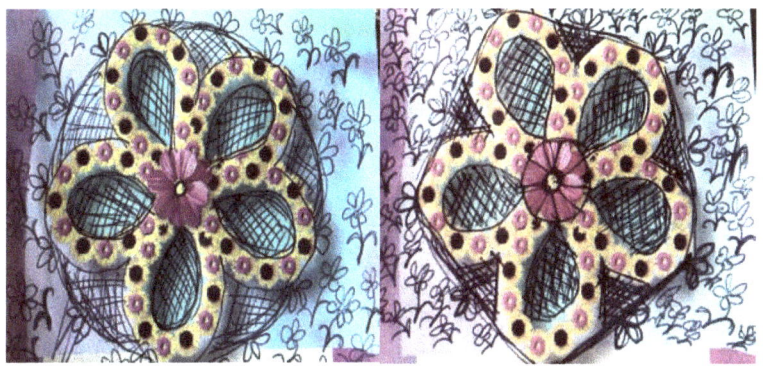

When you are listening to phone calls
but not focusing, you scribble.

You scribble, patterns of flowers
on the corner of newspapers, notepads
lying on the table.
Someday you draw a pentagon
sometimes a circle around the flower.
What you are thinking while drawing the patterns?
Maybe you are not thinking, your heart is directing
impervious of surroundings,
I wonder.

Like the flower, do you feel
sometimes bounded by a rigid structure
asymmetrical order inside the pentagon
and some other times feeling limitless,
blended in infinite symmetry of the circle,
I wonder.

Do we not dwell between those extremes
finite and infinite of our own making,
a struggle, continuous and never-ending.
Fragmented patterns, ignored before
now I keep it to understand more
your thoughts expressed in mysterious ways
scribbled in the corner of scratchpads.

July 2019

Midnight Poetry

I was half asleep switching between dreams,
when you came, in the wee hours of the night
You sat down, meditated for a while
before lying on the bed on my side.
I curled up towards you like a roly-poly;
my face touched your soft bosom valley.
warmth seeped like the fog of Golden Gate bridge
tried to sleep fluttering every few minutes like a butterfly
Finally, you murmured "Good night" and fell asleep.
I was wide awake; hamster in the circadian cycle.

Eyes awake, what else to do, no stars to look
I started noticing the rhythm in your breath
started slow but picked up as time went by
beating like Bolero music went up and down for a few minutes
the softness of your bosom, the cycle of beats in your heart
a perfect spot & time to think of the poetry of heart;
few lines of Pablo Neruda love poems flashed by
the longing conflicted emotions in Tagore's poems
imagined Gibran wondering in the street of Boston
I was lost where I was at that moment.

Like a baby bird fluttering in the nest
still feeling the warmth of closeness,
as I ruminate the thoughts in the poems; you flickered;
are you able to hear my voices within?
You are in deep sleep, I am awake, lying in bed
when day breaks, it seems we move far away.

Dancing moonlight seeping thru blinds, playing hide and seek
a burst of wind, clattering blinds, glaring moon wrapping
you flickered from your deep sleep; twisting to another side
murmured "good night" again, letting me out of the tight
I looked at the clock, 4 am alone and eyes open;
there is no better time to write the thoughts in a poem.

May 2020

Third eye

My mother said she prayed to Shiva
for six years, staying up nights for a child
to unshackle from the pressure of barrenness.
I was born on the seventh, I guess a blessed event!
When I was a child, I heard stories of Shiva;
glories from the mountains of Himalayas;
demons destroyed and battles fought.
When I became a young adult
I learned the power and oddities,
the opium to pacify and the nectar to save
the dancing damsels and the dance of death.
When I became an adult I questioned the dualities;
the women and Men, the creator and destroyer
the significant and contradictory acts.
Unanswered, unrevealed questions remain
yet, Shiva exists between present and emptiness.

In the years between youth and adulthood
age of innocence and self identification
dreams and imaginations raced along
I dreamt, I wished I had a third eye like Shiva
I would have the power to do good
like Phantom or Superman or Bahadur,
no one would touch me in school or elsewhere;
I could be popular with everyone, young and old
If only I had a third eye, I am the blessed one.
Dreams of youth, ignorant and foolish
now I know why it got vanquished
yet, like the sparks of extinguished fire
fragments remained in the heart.

Knowledge overtakes dreams in time
questioning the mythical meanings
a reflection of Shiva exists in every being
I am a part of it, realized or unrealized.
The third eye is there in me all along
I am blessed like all creatures big and small
It is there to destroy the ego and vanity
to enjoy the waves and nature in totality
beyond the confined fear of mortality.
Shiva, You have opened my third eye finally
yet my heart still beats for my mother dearly
for each Bel leaf, she gave to thee.

March 2019
(*) Bahadur is an Indian comic superhero that I grew up with.

Best Gift

What is the best gift I have gotten
I start to ruminate often
Is it something I got
or a wish in the thoughts
Is it a book read over and over
or written thoughts on paper.
Is it the tears when I became a father
or the words that were spoken in my ears
Is it some memory of past
like the stars, some faded some brighter.

I ask my shadow in the twilight
"What is the best gift we have shared"
tell me, Oh! me and not me
I am just a formless formed
a thumbprint in this vast ocean
I wait for the shadow to answer
like a dancer behind the curtain.

Darkness swallows the light
I understood my plight
It is there and not there
like a dancing wolf in the moonlight.
Silence forsaken the hidden
life dances in shadows unbidden.
Let the voice inside rise
listen to it in silence or otherwise
before the darkness swallows the light.

September 2018

Observations

Graduate

One by one, the dreamers line up
Marching forward like soldiers
a tussle on top, a beaming smile
even if the time seems uncertain
forget it for a while, march forward, rise up
young men and women, the world awaits!
Congratulations Graduates!

May 2019
[Watching my Son's graduation]

Community

We were a community united
even after we grew to hundreds
distance did not matter, we travelled together
meeting a few times a year blending new faces with older.
Now we are tribes along the temple boundaries
unlike the past, no marks on forehead to signify
yet invisible thoughts of division runs deep
we did not learn from the past, we have divided ourselves
the Gods laugh at us, "humans never understood us"
splintered, yet we keep looking to heaven
the clouds have moved on.

June 2019

Lockdown

Empty road, stranded cars
cold easterly winds blowing
scattered white cherry flowers
locked voices inside the home
winds murmuring; an eerie emptiness
Walking alone; am I in an alien movie?

The cafe is closing; tears rolling down my cheek
I work and live day by day
I am an illegal alien, struggling and inching;
what will I do now?
I ponder with the angst of next week and thereafter
Is an apocalypse on the horizon?
Mine seems to have started already
tears do not stop.

You can work from home, but I can't
I am the maid, cleaner, gardener
I am the one who fixes your house
I am struggling already like a stranded ship
fogged harbor, unknown destination,
why does this impact me much more?
I am in the bottom forty percent.

Oh, friend, I can not comfort you
in this hour of need
locked we are in these houses
yet that is what we need
to get the pandemic out of the way.
My thoughts are always with you

the difficult time will pass like always
the spring desert flowers await us.

There is hope, there is much hope
we are better off compared to centuries before
we have science and spirit to fight
we have the heart to help humanity
like the desert storms, the Tsunamis, the hurricanes
"This too shall pass," as Gandalf said.
We will rise again and say "It passed".

March 2020
Locked down inside house due to Covid-19

Airport

Rows and rows of expressionless faces
head lowered, unconcerned, busy with phones
A little boy glued to the glass window
jumps, every time a plane takes off
The simple sense of joy, have we forgotten?
Have we become zombies in silence?
The little boy has not stopped
I am the observer in silence
switching between the frames.

May 2019
(Chicago Airport)

Clue

A bird in flight
a poet not in sight
feel your heart
do not look afar
the clue is right there
flip your hand upright.

February 2018

Same Date

Today we are of the same age
but tomorrow is different.
Time has hammered each moment
but not the thoughts from yesterday
We meet again; mirrored destiny remains.

July 2017

Summer Afternoon

Lonely observer I am
in this deepest corner of self
lingering summer afternoon
anxious mind, anxious thoughts,
beating heart in rhythm
colors of imaginations
shadows of dreams
a test of patience
for a glance in between.
I wait. I wait.

The shadow of dreams slowly passes
flickering in the summer winds, oblivious
of the souls nearby souls of ignorance, souls of pain
marches slowly between frames.
Will everything be lost, when I stop observing
thoughts gets buried in trenches as it vanishes
I exist, I exist, a silent cry from within
a glance is all I need.
I wait again for the next day.

June 2017

Wave

I am a wave born in ocean, die in the beach
racing with wind by side
I carry an old bottle in the midst
a message of hope, I believe
a message of love, I believe
I am just a wave waiting for my fate
to crash in a rock or barren beach.
Will you be there to catch it?

July 2017

Destination

Waves bounce on the rocky shore again,
Winds slowly blow the scattered fall leaves,
Fire from the mountain top blinks and fades,
A traveller passes through the lingered mist,
A path unraveled, a new destination reached.

April 2019

Returned

You returned the gift, said need clarification,
puzzled; with the complexity yet unbroken,
an impromptu decision it was, that is all I can say
no deliberation, no entangled thoughts
few hundred pennies spent on bazaar on that day.
Yet you returned it for more clarifications;
what answers do I search from this vibration.
Next time, I will give you the red & yellow fall leaves
like you did in the cafe long before unraveling the mystery
no clarification needed, all explanations engraved in poetry.
The moment I leave, you can let the winds blow it away
I have kept mine.

November 2019

Anger

I have seen anger of my mother
but it lasts a few hours at most
I have seen anger of my father
it melts by the night dew drops
I have seen anger of my grandfather
It lasts until the morning walk to the rice fields
I thought I have seen all forms of anger
until one day you showed me yours
when I ignored your suggestion
put my interest ahead of others.
Still discovering you from the first phone call.

June 2019

Birthday

Every day millions of thoughts
born and die, I do not celebrate them.
Why I celebrate this ephemeral body
when deeds are what remains of me
Is it the glory that I leave behind
or the pain caused in between.
Why do I celebrate a day
where I had no role in that play?
It was a chance which caused it to happen
nothing more or nothing less.

February 2019

Death in Bed

Sitting in his office desk
a hundred year old farmer said,
"Soldiers and farmers do not die in bed",
Farmers dies in the field, soldiers in the battlefield,
the last breath sanctifies the land
where they have toiled and stand.

I am no farmer, I do not own any land
I am no soldier, no guns in my hand
yet, I will die in my own battlefield
to begin the new endless journey
seeds of love sprinkled along life's journey.

September 2018

Mind

The battlefield of the human mind is hard to understand
It is where Gods are born and demons are destroyed
what makes a thought a "GOD" and
what makes another a "DEVIL"
The shadow exists and light flickers.

February 2019

Thoughts

Thoughts spark like fireworks
mind and emotions play hide and seek
how do I calm it down?
Some say suppress the thoughts
some say ride along with it
some say take a deep breath.
I tried all these but failed miserably
Is there hope for me?

October 2018

Buddha

Buddha, the man
Buddha, the concept
Buddha, the path of enlightenment
Buddha, the fountain in the backyard
observing the cycle of water from a distance
there the magic in the flow waters
there is power in the serene pose
mind quiets with the sound of water drops
the lines of sculpture starts to blur
few moments of connectedness and then I flicker
What is Buddha, I question; the man, the teachings
or the voice from the water flowing in the fountain
the Buddha was there to teach me the moment
keep listening, sounds between droplets, empty spaces within.

July 2019

Thoughts

After I started going to the gym regularly every morning, I started observing two things: the early sunrise and the lonely palm tree. I thought to myself, if I take a minute to observe the same frame, it will help me navigate to find the right vibrations to my inner thoughts & feelings; help me understand my journey from its simplicity, the changing patterns and the empty space in between. This idea got extended during my early hikes also as I started to capture reflected thoughts. As I took the pictures, an idea came about to write the first thought in a few lines of poetry). The following poems reflect my thoughts - one minute of shared thoughts.

Before you read the poem, take a look at the picture, close your eyes for a minute and think - what thoughts and feelings cross your mind. It will be different - I have shared mine. Discover yours; we are all poets at heart!

Reflect and Enjoy!

I am the seeker in meditation
days and nights have gone
until the day when sky expanded
beyond the horizon
felt minuscule after what I saw
blenched by universal love
was it a moment of Nirvana
I am still standing here.

July 2019

Today, you are showing colors
blushing like a newlywed
I can sense the fragrance
the moon can wait.

July 2019

If there are paths to heaven
the clouds are my friends
one of them will carry me
to the point of no return.
All leads to the same beauty
no need to fight over it.

July 2019

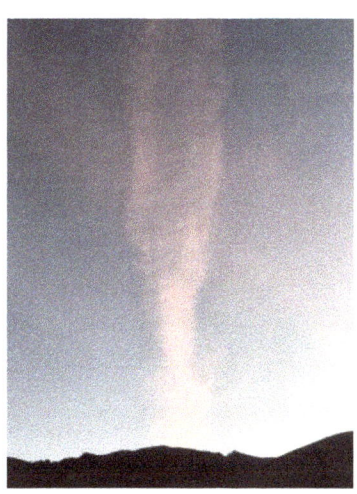

If Moses had seen it,
he would have understood
the message was from God.
When I saw it, I understood
behind obstacles, behind darkness
an unfathomable path exists
for the spirit to discover.
Moses found it; I am still searching.

July 2019

I see you blanched every morning
fragmented clouds, cold early sunrise
you have many admirers far and wide
I stand alone, unnoticed, yet I share
a minute of thought; that is all I have.

July 2019

We decorate temples and churches
with gold and glitters
admire the beautiful looks of the Gods
in return, we hope for the blessings.

Each day you are generous with different colors
blue, grey or pink blended with patterns
how do I thank you, for making the sky golden
I have nothing to offer beyond the minute of unspoken
each morning. Unshaken.

July 2019

Whenever I find myself in one corner;
you paint the sky.
I look for answers in your canvas of light and shades
sometimes I understand; many times it flashes by
I am not a painter, my canvas is still blank
fragments of yours are reflected in it for a few seconds.

October 2019

Between darkness and light, I stand
watching the messengers in flight.
dreams and hope, keeping alive.

July 2019

Sky has painted the canvas
to etch our thoughts of past
You are so far away
a faint smile is all I get.

July 2019

Standing alone day after day
I observed; different moods every day
until that day, what I saw
beyond imagination, bliss to anger,
I am fulfilled with the minute of love
I have longed for so long.

July 2019

Blessing from Desert Flowers

No trophies hang in my stead
no medals decorates in a case
no red carpet lies in-front when I walk
I have not achieved anything significant
I am just a commoner of humankind.

Yet, when I hike in the wilderness
flowers decorates the trail
red, blue, yellow, pink and purple
every season, I find a new color
in lowlands and high mountains
I can not name most of them
but I feel blessed when I see them.

I walk chest high, feeling content
a commoner of humankind
Yet, Mother Earth treats different
like every mother to her children
I am important in my Mother's eyes
and that's all it matters.

July 2019

Fog crawls slowly like a spider
caressing mountain, kissing trees
like the watch tower standing on top
am I watchful or lost in thoughts.

July 2019

The first time I saw you, crossing the Wowona Tunnel,
two words came about and both meant the same.
One word was for the amazing grandiose view
the other was for the sacredness of the realm,
a moment of silence, feeling the divine intent.

Every time I have visited since then
the same words still ring in my heart,
a place where eagle sores high
rainbow dances like newlywed
granite rocks stand erect, guardians
winds sing stories of past in silence
a place where Gods meets humans
a place humans realize the insignificance.

Yosemite, July 2019

Every winter, I come to see you
to put the crown in your head
to soothe the trampling of summer days
to listen to your stories of pain and joy
I am the snow, I am here again.

I am the one who protects you,
lets only worthy travelers pass by
fills the crevices with streams of water
smooths the rocks to shine again.
I am the snow; slowly melting away.

Without you holding me tight
I would not exist for long
in the whirling winds and in the cold rain
I am the snow, blessed by your kindness.

All alone I wait for the night to fall
under the starry sky to share the thoughts
we keep doing this dance year after year.
the stars are our promise keepers
I am there for you till the end
I am the snow, I am your friend.

July 2019

Sometimes, your reflection rejuvenates
like a painting on a canvas
sometimes, few squiggly lines surface
like a fainted smile, to cherish.
Everyday is new, when we meet
I let you draw until the end of light.
The shadow of darkness hides
the moon swims in the night.

July 2017

I asked the wooden path, does it go so far
beyond which, there is no turning back.
I stood for a moment in eerie silence, veered
no destination reached, yet I found a path.

July 2017

An empty road, a glorious sunrise
Alone in the car.
Known and unknown in front.
Audio on.
A talk explaining "Who am I?"
I switched it off.
Listen to the wind and silence.

August 2019

I am here everyday, waiting
basked in sunlight
caressed by moonlight
I am waiting for you;
sometimes you are in white
sometimes in blue,
sometimes angry and dark,
yet I like when you come near
letting go of your emotions in spurts
blanching the marks on travelled path
I am waiting everyday.

August 2019

Chatter and silence interspersed
in the darkness and sunlight
people waiting in lowlands
for the message to come; a path unraveled.

A ray of blue clouds drops like a veil
morning sun-rays glorifying the frame
they think, God may have finally spoken
coded messages written in the mountains
running like mad cows unearthing stones
to see the message written,
the silence is broken.

I call the wind to let them know
I am the same, the message is the same
Look inside, it is there, already written
I am just a mountain
I welcome everything with love and in silence.

August 2019

Between nothing and everything
a windless journey in silence
floating clouds, scattered dreams
a unrelentless badger searching
unaware, unfazed between rocks.
Have I become like him, mired by routine?
Have I stopped looking up for the empty spaces
except at the mountain top? I wonder.

Mt. Dana, July 2019

Blackbirds,
some say you are bad luck
yet I like to hear your voices
there is a stillness in truth
My day has just begun
I feel so welcomed!

July 2019

O Black Birds,
what did I say to startle you
I need you to carry the message
to the one I have been waiting
to hear, but do not get a reply
hear what I have to say!
O Black Birds!

July 2019

I fly alone between the shades
I am the blackbird of your dreams
I am no devil, the sky is cloudy and grey
I am no angel, the sky is bright and blue
I am the one talking to you every day
yet, a silence exists, enveloped
between the circles of fermented space.

March 2019

Don't be a stranger, O blackbirds!
the sky is pink, calmness engulfed
leaves are gone yet I am still here
one minute of you is all I ask
in between, we are strangers
the new leaves will sprout, I await.

July 2019

Wrath of Woolsey
ashed solitary column
memories sprinkle

December 2018 (Malibu)

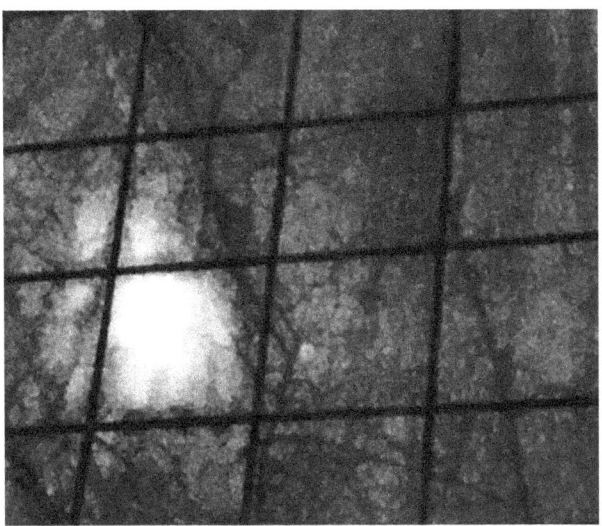

The branches have obscured your radiance;
scattered in frames like dreams
blanched in cold winter moonlight
unforgotten thoughts captured in frames.

July 2019

I have found myself in darkness
Yet, in the darkness, there is light
there is hope from the light
there is a path from the hope
From the darkness, there is light
I am the light!

July 2019

Memories afloat, blended in colors,
was it a chance or destiny, I wonder,
to meet in the strangest hours
a story etched in the labyrinth of venation,
still not forgotten;
the smile, like the dew from a leaf.

I visit the cafe to cross path again
you have moved on, I am still in pain.
Were you not the connected soul of dreams
unfathomable distance, a gorge of silence remains
dried crumpled red & yellow leaves, all that I have
between pages of poems, I have written.

July 2019

Shattered glass
blurred dreams
reflecting
fragmented self
unrecognizable
blended shadow
lurking
reminder of the self
stitch the infinite reflection,
complete the dream, a journey in making.

August 2019

I kept walking to sunset
did not realize footprints I left
I thank the desert, the preserver of stories
capturing memories in its heart
I thank the wind, the lover of silence
washing away blemishes engraved
The shadow is blurred. I walk to the sunset.

September 2019 (Dubai)

Reflections

Sunrise at Mt. Umunhum

Spring forward
let the clock move by an hour
an unceremonious event
to welcome the spring again.
I stand on top of Mt. Umunhum
a sacred land of long before
to feel the warmth of sunrise
to see the clouds below they rise.

On this land stands a radar tower
to watch for the invaders of war
It is a place to see the unseen
it is a place to connect within
it is a place to listen to voices afar
let the mind float in the air.
The spirit of natives still vibrates
the bravery of soldiers reverberates
reminding time is not in clock's hand
a battle exists in all sacred land
look no further than the mirror in hand.

March 2018

Mt Whitney

The darkness of summer stretched afar
A starless night, coldness biting
hissing wind, fluttering leaves
hikers with headlights, tapping spikes
a wooden gate, a small trail awaits
Is there a mountain behind the veil of darkness
imagination and anxiety, prevail.

Every step becomes harder
every breath becomes dearer
noise becomes silent
trees become distant
wind becomes friend
struggle brews between mind and body
body questions the forward move each time
spirit says few steps to heaven, continue
and then sunrise happens.

Switchback after switchback
ninety-nine of them, to climb only two thousand
life is like that, one turn after another
unknown becomes known then unknown
keep making the turns, life beacons
hours of the slow march to the mountaintop
few minutes to watch the view, that's all I got
I am alone in this vast painted view
a dot, dust, unknown traveler
barren mountains emptiness surrounds
climbing down, I lay my gratitude.
few footmarks I may have left
Mt Whitney, let the winds blow it away
few minutes of heaven, that's all I needed.

December 2018

Mount Kilimanjaro

In the land where apes evolved to sapiens,
where humans steps forged the new world
standing tall, touching the sky, watching
Mount Kilimanjaro, you have seen all,
O, mighty warrior of the realm.

Each day was different, from camp to camp
tropical forest flowers hiding in the labyrinth,
the groundsels of moorland watching like aliens;
the night sky to opens reminding oneself
a speck of dust we are in this unbounded space,
yet, one feels secure traversing your land.
The volcanic stones sprouts to the sky
each imprinted with stories, ready to tell
I have come to listen to what you have to say
a few footprints I leave in the process.

Each step in the darkness seems like a struggle
as we marched in a single file to the top
space between the breaths becomes apparent
a search of oneself happens in those empty moments.
The demons of altitude tricking the mind constantly
numb fingers and toes came alive with beautiful sunrise
I saw your majestic peak shining and felt blessed
fragments of glaciers scattered across reminiscent
you looked so near yet it took hours to reach to the top
you helped me all along with your stories hissing in my ears.

I went as a hiker with a goal to reach the top;
I left knowing myself a bit better in the process
your love in my heart and stories of your past to tell
Ashante Sana Kilimanjaro, O mighty warrior of the realm.

After hiking to Mount Kilimanjaro in September, 2019.

Persimmon Tree

In an old man's front yard, every fall
the Persimmon tree stands tall
laden with fruits from top to bottom
no one to pluck and hand them.
I wish I could see the old man this evening
to help him enjoy his own making.
I wait for him as I enjoy the sight
unchained gates do not invite.
Like a dream in flight
shadows outshine the light.
I stand and stare
laughing at my struggled affair
of Persimmons that seem so far
be it the old man's home or
in my backyard.

Once in two years, I wait for you
but squirrels eat it before I get to you
a struggle brews
new techniques used
to save a few
but squirrels get to it
no matter what I do.
One day my neighbor got a cat
the squirrels seem to have noticed that
the squirrels still mince on the fruits from the top
and leave the bottom ones for us to plop
and that's a lucky break I got.

December 2017

Water Connection

Every three days, sprinklers work in rhythm
few minutes of water to keep the plants in motion
The story in my backyard is quite different
the sprinklers break so often, gave up fixing them
rely on the age old pipe of twists and turns,
water all the plants every few days in the evening sun.

Unlike my front yard,
I know the plants; from big to small
as I water them circling along the fence wall.
The passion flower tree has crawled all over
with a canopy of flowers on the tree top
The succulents are spreading fast
a collection from many desert parks.

Squirrels seem to have taken a break,
at last few persimmons hanging for our sake!
I give extra water to the flowering plants
where hummingbirds gather one by one
amazing to see them flickering everyday
visiting all the plants in their buzzing way.
I notice which plants will flower soon
trimming between the cycles of moon
they all have voices in bare
unnoticed in silence we share.
I am glad that the sprinkler stopped working
even if it has caused me more suffering
I feel more connected to all of them
the few seconds I spend with them.

So many social channels to communicate
automated replies and unintended consequences.
Many "HBD" messages I get for sure
do they mean much, except scroll faster.
Like the plants in the backyard, I do it now;
water the connections, to the people I know
make that call and do a bit chatter
those few seconds do matter.

December 2018

Window

A glass pane window
a maple tree
a hummingbird
a stranded soul
a world of divide,
one free spirit
one locked inside.
Like an old man, I sit near the window
fighting the fever and flu alone
mind wonders beyond the pane
even if the body is in pain
I can hear the sound of thunder
I can imagine the touch of wind
I can sense the freshness of rain
but twenty four square feet divides
between imagination and chain.

Enclosed in a geodesic dome
windows of vanity and self pity
words do not break
sound do not cross
thoughts bounce in the hollowed dome
struggle brew in cascades,
to hear the hummingbird
to touch falling yellow and red leaves
to feel the raindrops
to sense the cool breeze
before shattered windows dissolve
the dust becomes dust!

October 2018

Beyond the end point

Confluence by an ocean and two seas
an endpoint of my old country
a lonely rock two thousand yards in the sea
hundred years ago, a soul sat and meditated
he could look beyond the endpoint
found answers inspired millions.

Standing at the rock, the view is wide
bodies of water on all three sides
sunrise and sunset are glorious each day
one can only meditate in this beautiful place
what do I see beyond the endpoint, I question

The northerly east wind blows in swirls
palm trees doing their dance in curls
the birds circling over from land to sea
a church, a mosque and a temple near the beach
each one asserting with voices of heaven
What do you claim at this endpoint?
I pondered myself standing at this point
what exists inland, merges with the ocean
what brews in ocean migrate to the land
the cycle exists and will exist
I am just a small part of it
there is no "end" in this endpoint
I will be in the ocean at some point.

January 2019
Kanyakumari is the end point of India.
Swami Vivekananda meditated on the rock before he headed to Chicago in 1893.

Traditions

Today there is an uproar in the state
two young women dared to enter the temple
where only men and old women could enter.
"The God could be lured by young damsels", men say
that is the tradition why women were barred to pray,
then Gods are no better than Men, desire stricken
Men are worse than Gods, rules we do not question
traditions need to change.

One black woman dared to sit in the front
white men made an uproar, violent acts followed
not to break the traditions of blinded racism
struggled brewed, thousand died
equality, a struggle still inflame
traditions need to change!

Few women marched in the long silence
to make it count in existence.
Men cajoled, why do it now, go back to the kitchen
thousands marched, for the voting rights
hundred years of struggle still in the fight
many places women cannot vote yet
why women are constrained by the society of men
traditions need to change!

Few women dared to speak of the past
advantage men took while at work
#MeToo movement made a statement
some say it was about time for the change
some said it went too far, not sure if it is needed

have you thought about the women in pain
traditions need to change!
So many inequalities for thousands of years
it may be religious pretext or judgment uproar
why women had to take so much burden
constraints for every occasion, chained
traditions need to change!
Each of us needs to take a stand, Men and Women
break the old traditions which do not make sense
when my grandfather died, the priest told rules in religious text
bereaved women should not do "this and that"
all sorts of constraints, to make her life more painful
the text had very little for the Men if it happened differently
"forget what scriptures rules", I am ignorant
will look after my grandmother, she is already in pain.
"Love" trumps all traditions, that is all we understand
traditions need to change
traditions in inequalities MUST change!

January 2019
Kerala, India - Day of Sabrimala temple strike.

Celebrations: Circle of Life (Nuakhai)

Row one / adult men sitting cross-legged on mats
impatient, checking the clock for the auspicious moment.

Row two / children sitting in a big line front
some giggling and some uncomfortable by the acts of cousins.

Row three / half of the women sitting towards the end of the veranda
close to the kitchen & half still busy with preparing food items.

The men, children, and women from the oldest to the youngest in sequence
everyone dressed new for this occasion to welcome the new harvest, new year
stretched hands holding the new rice prepared with milk and honey
sprinkled basil leaves on top, reminiscent of Gods offering
waiting for the auspicious moment to arrive
stretched hands waiting.
Everyone takes a moment of silence
followed by a small prayer by the eldest
bless the Mother Earth
bless the Sun
bless the Winds
bless the Monsoon Rain
bless the Rice Plants
the seeds they carry will carry us forward
Om Peace Peace!

One by one, we eat the sweet delicacy in unison
the circle of life begins with the new season
each person bow to elders one by one
a blessing from them to complete the final dance.

June 2019

Poetry & Wine

I wrote a few lines of poetry
friends said, "You have become a poet";
I drank a few glasses of wine
friends said, "You have become a tippler";
"Poetry is like wine", a famous poet and I say
once you taste it, you never turn back.
Poetry stays inside the deepest corners of heart
like wine inside a bottle waiting to be served;
sometimes agonizes, sometimes makes you laugh
in the flickering shadows of the moon during the wee hours.

This body is like an old tavern
a cup for wine and a line of poetry is heaven
thirsty mind, thirsty heart calls again and again
for a few drops to quench the longing ingrained.
Bring me something - I can wait no longer
pacify the agonizing heart crying over and over;
I am not worried what you will you get
Poetry or Wine, I see no difference.

November 2017
("Poetry is like Wine" - R L Stevenson)

River banks

River banks - paired existence
comes closer but never meet
the ocean swallows in the end for eternity.
River banks - chained lovers in waiting
with the morning sun and evening wind
with the moonlight and the darkness in between
for the floods to come before the end
to renew the memories for few moments
to gather the dust from past to present;
seasons after seasons pass by, waiting never ends.

Flood - the wind of lovers
eclipses the river banks
wipes away the longing for few moments;
love and water do the same
remove the barriers, we need to understand.
For now the two banks wait,
imprisoned by cycle of time;
for the wind and flood to come again
to meet one more time.

Like the river bank, I am also waiting
waiting, with the winds and rain
with the red & yellow fall leaves in hand
for few moments to meet again
connect past and present
share what was lost and gained
but there is no flood - waiting never ends.

Now, time has engulfed past and present
barren voices surrounds the realm
what was a river, what was a bank
now lost forever in the dunes of sand
Like the river which leaves marks hidden
I also have left few lines of poetry
inscribed in the grains of sand.

October 2017

Line in the sand

We draw lines
often, on the spur
in the shadow of anger
in the shadow of emptiness
between breaths of emotions
We stay silent
for years to come
We repent
but we are not brave enough
We suffer, not knowing
lines are in the sand
wind can erase it
waves can erase it
stroke of palm can erase it
words can erase it
so simple yet we forget
when we draw the line
its is always in the sand.
I have removed mine.

December 2018

Strange Number

I woke up in the middle of a cold winter night
a number flashed in the dream twilight
I pondered what that could be
Is it a passage number from the scripture
to get an answer to questions from days before
or a page number of the book I love
or the date of a letter I wrote
or a divine hint to go and buy a lottery
or random thoughts at night, should I worry.

I tried all kinds of tricks to understand
googled it and did some complex math
date of birth, pin codes, passwords, social security,
grades, scores of past, and connections in obscurity
but no luck! It was a simple number
not as big as Avogrado or Aleph naught
not as beautiful as topological dimensions
I wondered if its existence in my consciousness
a simple three digit number with no providence.

Not able to find its significance
all I can think of now
my heart may know it's a reminiscence
hope that its vibrations have spread its wings
my quest continues to find its meaning
what is lost may lead to a new beginning
the number was "2?3", let you keep guessing
It still comes back once in a while
for me to continue to search even in futility.

December 2018

Life

Life
I have mine
you have yours
yet how do I define it
many questions still exists
between the windless dreams
between silent water navigating river banks
between splashing waves rocking every second
an intertwined thought, a reflection
fluttering sound of hummingbird
the swings of myriad thoughts
yet I await for answers
you have yours
I have mine
mortality
ends.

March 2019

Basket of Prayers

You said you prayed tonight, prayed not for yourself
for souls knowing; a prayer for each
from your prayer basket.

I closed my eyes and thank for thee
sun and clouds playing hide and seek
northerly wind silently hissing the trees
pages of "Mystery of Leaves" book fluttering
crumbled yellow and red leaves saved in pages;
now brown, slowly floating with the winds.

The leaves are gone; imprints remain
remains in the pages, in the heart
like a prayer.

Have I been in your basket of prayer?
these words would not flow
this journey would not continue
this wandering soul once stranded in the mirage
would not have found the unspoken thoughts,
without the tears and prayers guiding through.

Have you put yourself in the basket of prayers?
If you have not, allow me to stretch my thoughts
put the imprinted leaf pages in the basket of prayers
touch your heart, answers you seek will be in the prayers.

April 2020

God of Experience

Experience the God
Every Swami, priest, mystic says
But there are thousands of them
God of fire, God of wine, God of War
God of Knowledge, God of War
One God, My God, True God
Gods - human creations.
Do they tip the balance?
I am search of the God of experience
experience, seed of consciousness
experience, the thread binding
past & present, limiting and limitless
What should I do now?
I live, I experience, I am conscious
I am the God of my own experience…
I experience the "self".

June 2019

Dilemma

A window, a door, a closet, a table
elements of a room framed in daily routine
unnoticed relationships in existence
hours spent in the emptiness of oneself
working, reading, observing the birds in the trees
seeing passion flowers opening with the sunlight
sitting in meditation for few minutes facing the closet
where statues of Gods reside arranged in altar perfect
where my father did his daily prayer when he was here
where my mom lit the incense with care
where I sit with family listening to the chants
work and love filled this rectangular cuboid.

Once I sat down for meditation
early morning light twinkling through the blinds
thousands of thoughts running in my mind
suddenly, a thought hit me like a lightning
I am facing the window and the altar is behind
have I committed a wrongful act - I questioned
should I turn 180 degrees, a dilemma ran in my mind
in the middle of a meditative moment, breaking the
silence within.

I reflected over few minutes of the dilemma I faced
I have seen people taking selfies in temples and churches
images of God behind them with smile on their face
I used to question the ignorant act, I must say
not anymore, I have realized I do the same act
taking selfies when I climbed mountains
the divine is everywhere beyond my limiting dimensions

we have limited the Gods and ourselves to the narrow road
let the barriers go, let the divine reflection
shine through our minds
like the moon reflecting sunlight
the window in the room is the gateway to the heart
the door in the room is the escape route of the soul
the closet is the room is the mind where God reside
the table in the room facing window where inner thoughts arise
I did the right thing not turn one hundred eighty degrees
let the thought pass by, I am just a dust in making
I close my eyes to welcome a new thought to shine.

February 2019

Engraved Thoughts

Traveler checks, a thing of past
but some memories do last.
encashing them was a challenge
in this remote home town, I visited often
It was a day long affair to the lonely bank
sit with the manager for hours under the cranky fan
the teller keeps writing the long numbers
one by one, engraving in the ledger
I admired his passion or tactics to get some favor.

Now it is so easy to use cards and mobile
the economist will say, the market is more liquid
to grow, make the flow unconstrained.
My mind is like a marketplace
thoughts travel like currencies, faster than light
some created by me and some from external stimuli
it spans the full spectrum
from good to bad, known to unknown, shared to hidden
some vanishes quickly, some resists
the one I resist, agonize, makes me go slow
wish I could quickly let them flow
not engrave each of them like the teller
ruminating it over and over letter by letter
let each thought travel absolved.

December 2018

Audience of One

We are humans.
We, humans, are poets at heart.
We are poets in search of an audience.
I have found one.

O audience of One
I am just a poet in making
locked words before, now surfacing.
We are unknown, in the unending dreams
mirage of my poems - I am imagining.

O audience of One
do not be a "fan" of my poems
the winds of your wishes will blow me away
do not be amber to the words of my poems
the fire from you will burn me to ashes
do not smile too much as you read between the lines
the thoughts of you will make me daydream
do not look too intensely searching between the waves
the depth of your eyes will drown me unengraved.

O audience of One,
I am on a journey in the sailing winds of life
let me exist for a few moments between
the reminiscent smiles and glancing eyes;
blended shadows reflected in the mirror of memories.
Like a leaf floating, I exist in your waves;
and you in my poems - O audience of One!

May 2020

Poetic winter

I find myself in a poetic winter
words come slowly than before
I have listened to the waves of ocean
I have walked with the trees
I have climbed the mountains
alone
for the words which did not exist before.
The sunrise and the sunset
the red and yellow leaves of fall
the tumbleweed and squirrels
the summer winds and cold winters
have clenched the soul.
Now, I have come down from the hill
with the depth of emotions are filled
but as long as I
can listen to the sound birds
feel hissing wind of the yellow leaves
can hear the unspoken words
can see the shadows of moon
feel the warmth of the flicker of light
I will be a poet in heart
even if the words come no more!

February 2018

Atheist

The temples do not call me anymore
the mountains do.
The rhythm of chanting do not speak to me
but the silence of mountains do.
The smell of incense do not make me meditate
but each step in the dusty hiking path does.
I do believe in the divine forces of universe
I am an insignificant drop
in the vastness of ocean
a dust in the peaks of mountain
an epoch in the cosmic grandeur
unfathomable beyond imagination.
I still go to temples for my social obligation
bow to few idols and listen to few songs
but once I leave, no experience stays with me
except the beautiful architecture and history.

The mountain welcomes all
unlike the halls of temple and synagogue
caste and color, local or foreigner do not matter
after all, we all are from the same color
indistinguishable dusts off mother earth.
No need to listen to a priest or rabbi
listen to the cool breeze, the learnings are hidden
message of hope rides with each ray of sunrise
love floats in the air, touch the gentle falling leaves
What is more divine than this?

Yes, I have become an atheist
the religious rituals do not speak
my friends and family may not agree
I say, find a path of divinity to attain
like I did with blessings from mountains
I will not judge as you discover
dust will become dust
as we take the journey together.

November 2018

A Letter To Myself

What should I write to myself, if I have to?
it is not the last letter before the sunset
so, no moral storms or words of guilt,
or lines of wisdom to write;
so what should write to myself, I pontificate.

A breeze rattles the blinds as I stare
blank computer screen for words to appear.
Should I write a letter of failings and dark thoughts
or should I glorify myself stretching the truth
or should I write about things I have done
or should write about loved ones
or write things I have yet to do
Who am I, I have yet to discover,
where will I go, there is no answer,
what would I write, I ponder
a letter to "I' from "me", I wonder.
Eyes roll across the white walls over and over
a black and white MLK poster says,
"If you have not discovered something…"
I start to ponder, have I found anything to live for.

"Do not look for a path, you are on a desert
anywhere you go, you will create the path,
no need to worry if people will follow you
winds will blow it away, you are in a desert.
Write poetry, even if no one reads; they are for you
captured thoughts sprinkled in the labyrinth of oneself.
Listen to the mountains as you hike
like, mothers, they do not discriminate
it is where, one discovers oneself.

Let your thoughts of loved ones reflect
with sunrise, a minute is all that takes.
No one will remember your glories
you have achieved none; so do not pursue it.
Experience life like wind - smell the wind.
Listen to the water; be like water
polish few stones along life's journey
that is all to realize in one's own making.
Be like water - polish a few stones"

That is all I have to say to myself,
"I am the snow. I am the water,
polish few stones, that's all it matters",
I have discovered something to live for.

October   2019

Photograph by Vas Bhandarkar

A hiker, biker, nature lover dabbling in poetry once in a while, Prasanta lives in California, USA. His first poetry book *"Mystery of Leaves"* was published in 2017.

www.ingramcontent.com/pod-product-compliance
Lightning Source LLC
Chambersburg PA
CBHW042127100526
44587CB00026B/4199